Ribticklers

Robert Swindells
Anne Fine
Terence Blacker

Ribticklers

Contents

What's for Dinner?......... 5
by Robert Swindells
illustrated by Fred Blunt

Crummy Mummy............ 21
by Anne Fine
illustrated by Francis Blake

Karate for Kids............ 43
by Terence Blacker
illustrated by Kevin February

What's for Dinner?
by Robert Swindells

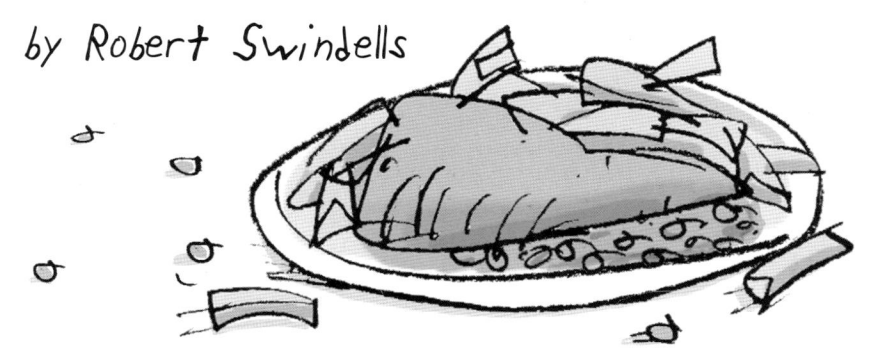

"It's Friday," Sammy Troy complained. "Fish and chip day. Why are we landed with shepherd's pie?"

"I don't know, do I?" said Jane. They were twins, but Sammy was ten minutes younger and ten years dafter. Jane spent half her time at school keeping him out of trouble. She swallowed a forkful of the pie. "It's very tasty anyway. Try it."

Sammy tried it. It was excellent, but he wasn't going to admit it. He'd been eagerly anticipating fish and chips, and shepherd's pie just couldn't compare. He pulled a face.

"Pigfood."

"Don't be silly," said Jane, but she knew he would be. He usually was.

Sammy left most of his dinner, and in the playground afterwards he composed a rap. It was about the school cook, and it went like this:

> *Elsie Brook is a useless cook.*
> *If you eat school dinners, it's your hard luck.*
> *They'll either kill or make you ill.*
> *If the meat don't do it then the custard will.*

It wasn't true. Mrs Brook did good dinners, but the rap caught on and a long snake of chanting children wound its way about the playground with Sammy at its head. Jane didn't join in. She thought it was stupid and prayed Mrs Brook wouldn't hear it.

On Saturday, Sammy practised the rap with some of his buddies. They intended to get it going again at break on Monday, but at the end of morning assembly, the Head said, "I'm sorry to have to tell you all that our Mrs Brook was taken ill over the weekend, and will not be here to cook for us this week."

Some of the boys grinned and nudged one another. Sammy whispered in Jane's ear "She must've eaten some of that shepherd's pie." Jane jabbed him with her elbow.

"However," continued the Head, "we are very lucky to have with us Mr Hannay, who will see to our meals till Mrs Brook returns. Mr Hannay is not only a first-class chef, but an explorer as well. He has travelled as cook on a number of expeditions to remote regions, and is famous for his ability to produce appetizing meals from the most unpromising ingredients."

"He'll feel at home here, then," muttered Sammy. "We have the most unpromising ingredients in Europe."

A chef, though! A first-class chef. Morning lessons seemed to drag on forever. It felt like three o'clock when the buzzer went, though it was five to twelve as always. Hands were washed in two seconds flat, and everybody scurried along to the dining area, which was filled with a delicious mouth-watering aroma. Snowy cloths covered all the tables, and on each table stood a little pot of flowers. "Wow!" breathed Jeannette Frazer. "It's like a posh restaurant."

And the food. Oh, the food. First came a thick, fragrant soup which was green but tasted absolutely fantastic. To follow the soup there was a beautiful main course – succulent nuggets of tender white meat in a golden, spicy sauce with baby peas and crispy roast potatoes. For pudding there were giant helpings of chocolate ice cream with crunchy bits in it.

Sammy licked the last smear of ice cream from his spoon, dropped the spoon in his dish, pushed the dish away and belched. Some of the boys giggled, but his sister glared at him across the table. Sammy smirked. "Sorry, but what a meal, eh? What a stupendous pig-out. I'll probably nod off in biology this aft."

He didn't though. Miss Corbishley didn't give him the opportunity. The class was doing pond life, and when they walked in the room the teacher said, "Jane and Sammy Troy, take the net and specimen jar, go down to the pond, and bring back some pond beetles and a water boatman or two. Quickly now."

The school pond lay in a hollow beyond the playing field. Rushes grew thickly round its marshy rim and there were tadpoles, newts and dragonflies as well as sticklebacks and the beetles they'd study today. It was Sammy's favourite spot, but today all the creatures seemed to be hiding. No dragonflies darted away as the twins waded through the reeds. No sticklebacks scattered like silver pins when Jane trawled the net through the pondweed, and when she lifted it out it was empty.

"Try again," said Sammy. Faster."

Jane sent the net swooping through the underwater forest, but all she got was a plume of weed.

"Everything seems to have vanished," she said. "And Miss is waiting."

"I know," said Sammy. "She'll think we've wagged off school."

"Don't be ridiculous!" cried Miss Corbishley, when Jane told her there was nothing in the pond.

"Only this morning Mr Hannay was saying what a well-stocked pond we have at Milton Middle."

The twins were sent to their seats in disgrace, while Jeannette Frazer and Mary Bain went to try their luck. Miss Corbishley made a giant drawing of a water boatman on the board and the children began copying it into their books.

"Hey, Jane!" hissed Sammy. His sister looked up. He had a funny expression on his face. "I've just had a thought."

"Congratulations," she whispered. "I knew you might some day."

"No, listen. You know what Miss said, about Mr Hannay?"

"What about it?"

"He said the pond was well stocked, right? And we had that fantastic dinner, only we didn't really know what was in it?"

"What's dinner got to do with – ?" Jane broke off and gazed at her brother. "No, Sammy. No. That's sick. It's impossible."

"Is it?" Sammy jabbed a finger at her. "What was that

soup then? Green soup ... and the meat ... and those crunchy bits in the ice cream – what were they?"

Before Jane could reply, Jeannette and Mary returned with long faces and an empty jar.

Walking home that afternoon, Jane said, "It's a coincidence, that's all. It can't be true what you're thinking, Sammy." She wasn't sure, though, and Sammy certainly wasn't convinced. "I wonder what we'll get tomorrow," he said.

Tuesday's dinner turned out to be every bit as delicious as Monday's. The twins had kept their suspicions to themselves, so there were no spoilt appetites as the children settled down to eat. Even Jane and Sammy felt better. After all, even Mr Hannay couldn't conjure food from an empty pond.

The soup was orange and there were no lumps in it. It had plenty of flavour, though, and everybody enjoyed it. The main course was Italian – mounds of steaming pasta and a rich, meaty tomato sauce. "If this is how they eat in Italy," said Sammy, "I'm off to live there." He seemed to have forgotten about yesterday. Jane hadn't, but she knew macaroni when she saw it, and this was definitely macaroni.

Tuesday afternoon was CDT with Mr Parker. When the kids arrived he was kneeling in front of his big cupboard, surrounded by a mountain of dusty old drawings, and broken models made from balsa wood and cardboard boxes. "Lost something, sir?" enquired Sammy.

Mr Parker nodded. "I'm afraid I have, lad. I could've sworn they were in here."

"What, sir?"

"Some pictures I did with a first-year class, three, maybe four, years ago. Collage pictures."

"What are they, Sir?"

"Oh, you know – you stick things on a sheet of paper to make a picture. Seashells, lentils, bits of macaroni. Any old rubbish you can find, really."

Sammy gulped. "Bits of macaroni, sir?"

"That's right."

"Four years ago, sir?"

"Yes. I'm sure I saw them at the back of this cupboard quite recently. I made a mental note to clear them out before the mice got to them."

"Are there many mice in your cupboard, sir?" There was a greenish tint to Sammy's face.

"Oh yes, lad. Mice, moths, woodlice, cockroaches. The odd rat, probably. It's a miniature zoo this cupboard."

Sammy didn't enjoy CDT that afternoon. He couldn't

concentrate. He kept picturing old Hannay in his blue and white striped apron, rooting through Parker's cupboard.

When he glanced across at Jane, he thought she looked unwell. He wondered how Mrs Brook was getting along, and when the boys did the rap at break he didn't join in.

On Wednesday, Jane and Sammy decided they wouldn't eat school lunch unless they knew what it was. Sammy said "How do we find out what it is?"

"We ask," Jane told him. At ten o'clock she stuck her hand up and asked to go to the toilet but went to the kitchen instead. Mr Hannay wasn't there, but Mrs Trafford was. "Where's Mr Hannay?" asked Jane. She hoped he'd left, but Mrs Trafford said, "He's just slipped along to the gym, dear. Why – who wants him?"

"Oh, nobody," said Jane. "I was wondering what's for dinner, that's all."

"Opek," replied Mrs Trafford.

"Pardon?" said Jane.

"Opek. It's a very old, oriental dish, Mr Hannay says. Very nice."

15

Opek turned out to be a grey, porridgy mush. It didn't appear all that promising, but it was probably what ancient oriental grub was supposed to look like, and it tasted fine.

Everybody was enjoying it till Gaz Walker fished a small flat rectangular object from his plate and held it up.

"Here," he complained. "Why is there a Size 4 tag in my dinner?"

"Let's have a look." Jane took the tag and examined it. It resembled the sort of tag you'd find inside a shoe.

"Opek," she murmured, wondering why Mr Hannay had been in the gym when he was supposed to be cooking. "Opek." An idea formed in her head and sank slowly into her stomach where it lay like a lead weight. She put the tag on the rim of her plate and sat back with her hands across her stomach. All round the table, kids stopped eating and watched her.

"What's up, Jane?" Sammy's voice was husky.

"Opek," whispered Jane. "I think I know what it means."

"What?" asked Jeannette, who had almost cleared her plate.

"I think it's initials," said Jane. "Standing for Old PE Kit."

The peace of the dining area was shattered by cries of revulsion and the scrape and clatter of chairs, as everybody on Jane's table stampeded for the door. The kids at the other tables watched till they'd gone, then lowered their heads and went on eating opek.

Sometimes two people can keep a secret, but never ten. There were ten kids at Jane and Sammy's table, and so the secret was revealed. Nobody went into dinner on Thursday. Nobody. At twelve o'clock, Mr Hannay raised the hatch and found himself gazing at twelve empty tables. He frowned at his watch. Shook it. Raised it to his ear. At five past twelve, he took off his apron and went to see the Head. They stood at the Head's window, looking towards the playing field. All the children were there, and some seemed to be eating the grass. "Good lord," sighed the Head. "What did you cook, Hannay?"

"Epsatsc," said the chef.

"Never heard of it," said the Head. "Whatever is it?"

"Traditional Greek dish," said Hannay smoothly, easily fooling the Head. Jane, who'd got the word from Mrs Trafford, wasn't fooled. "Epsatsc," she said grimly, leaning on a goal post. "Erasers, pencil shavings and the school cat."

On Friday everybody brought sandwiches, but they needn't have because Hannay had gone and Mrs Brook was back. When they spotted her crossing the playground at five to nine, the kids cheered. Mrs Brook, who was the sentimental type, had to wipe her eyes before she could see to hang up her coat. The kids chucked their butties into the bin and Sammy's rap was dead.

Dinner wasn't fish and chips, but there were no complaints. Everybody tucked in with gusto – even Sammy. The snowy cloths had gone and there were no flowers, but there was something else instead. Contentment. You could feel it all around.

And so the school week drew to a close. Everybody relaxed. The work was done. The weekend, bright with promise, lay ahead. At half past three the kids spilled whooping into the yard and away down the drive. Jane and Sammy, in no rush, strolled behind. At the top of the drive stood the gardener, looking lost. Sammy grinned.

"What's up, Mr Tench?" The gardener lifted his cap and scratched his head. "Nay," he growled. "There were a pile of nice, fresh horse manure here this morning and it's gone."

The twins exchanged glances. Mrs Brook was coming down the drive. They ran to her. "Mrs Brook!" cried Sammy. "That Mr Hannay – he has left, hasn't he?"

The cook nodded. "Yes, dear. I'm afraid he has, but don't worry – he left me his recipe book. You know it's just amazing the meals you can get out of stuff you find lying around."

20

Crummy Mummy

by Anne Fine

I don't consider my mum's fit to be a parent, really I don't. Every morning it's the same, every single morning. I'm standing by the front door with my coat on, ready to go. School starts at nine, and it's already eight-forty or even later, and she's not ready. She's not even nearly ready. Sometimes she isn't even dressed.

"Come *on*," I shout up the stairs. "We have to leave now."

"Hang on a minute!"

"What are you *doing* up there?"

Her voice comes, all muffled, through the bedroom door:

"Nothing."

"You *must* be doing something," I yell.

"I'm *not*."

"Come down, then. We're *waiting*."

"Can't find my shoes."

I lean against the front door, sighing. With as much patience as I can muster, I call upstairs:

"Where did you take them off?"

"I *thought* I took them off in the bathroom ..."

"Look there, then."

"I *have*."

"If you would only put your shoes away neatly at night, we wouldn't have to go through this every single morning!"

By now, of course, my baby sister's fretting. She's strapped inside her pushchair and, since I put her coat and bonnet on at least ten minutes ago and she's still indoors, her head and ears are getting hot and scratchy. She's boiling up into one of her little rages. Already she's trying to tug her bonnet off. "Will you come *on*?" I shout upstairs.

"I'm coming. I'm coming!"

"Well, hurry *up!*"

At last, she comes downstairs. Even then she's never dressed right. You'd think, honestly you would, that we didn't have any windows upstairs, the way she chooses what to wear. She certainly can't bother to look through them at the weather. She'll sail down in midwinter, when it's snowing, in a thin cotton frock with short puffy sleeves, and no woolly.

I have to be firm.

"You can't come out like that."

"Why not?"

"You just can't," I tell her. You'll catch your death. It's snowing out there. It's *far* too cold for bare arms. You'll freeze."

"I'll put a coat on."

But I just stare at her until she goes back upstairs for a sweater. And even then she'll choose something quite unsuitable. She never dresses in the right sort of thing. She'd wear her glittery legwarmers to a funeral if I let her (or if we ever went to funerals). She'd sit on a beach in her thick purple poncho. If she were called in to see the headmaster, she'd rather wear those baggy flowery shorts she found abandoned on a park bench last Easter than anything sensible. She'd look fantastic — she always does — but not at all like a mother. You have to watch her. You can't let up.

At least she admits it.

"I'm a terrible embarrassment to you, Minna," she confesses, buckling on two of her best studded belts. "I'm a Crummy Mummy."

Then I feel mean for being so stern.

"You're not a Crummy Mummy," I tell her. "You do your best. And I suppose it doesn't *really* matter what you look like …"

"You're right," she says, cheering up at once. And then, if you let her, she'd get worse. At least, that's what my gran says, and she should know because she's her mother.

I like my gran. She lives right on the other side of the estate, but she comes over almost every teatime. She picks Miranda out of the cot, and coos to her, and then she sits with Miranda on her knee on the only bit of the sofa that isn't leaking stuffing. Mostly, she tells Mum off.

She says now Mum's a mother of two, it's time she grew up and pulled herself together. She tells Mum she should throw all her safety-pin earrings and lavender fishnet tights into the dustbin, and go out and buy herself a nice, decent frock from Marks and Spencers. She says Mum ought to take those horrible Punk Skunks records off the stereo before they ruin Miranda, and put something nice and easy to listen to, like Perry Como's Christmas Selection.

And then, if Mum hasn't already flounced off in a huff, Gran purses her lips together as if she's been sucking lemons and, clutching Miranda so tightly her dummy pops out of her mouth and her face goes purple, she whispers to Mum that she's clearly still very much under the influence of that dreadful, *dreadful* –

Here, she looks around shiftily, and drops her voice even lower:

"I don't even want to say his *name* in front of the innocent children, but you know exactly who I mean."

I know exactly who she means, too. She means Crusher Maggot, that's who she means.

Crusher Maggot is Mum's boyfriend. It was me who first called him Crusher Maggot because that's what he looks like, and when he first started coming round here I didn't like him. Now I like him a lot, but it's too late. The nickname's stuck. He doesn't mind, though. Now even Mum calls him Crusher Maggot.

Gran disapproves of Crusher. She thinks he's a very bad influence on Mum. She blames him for giving Miranda her nickname – Crummy Dummy – and she particularly hates his hair. She says it's a hideous embarrassment.

Crusher's hair is fantastic. He even won a punk hair competition with it once, and his photo ended up on one of those London postcards that tourists send home to their friends for a laugh. The postcard was called *London's Burning* and there's our Crusher, teeth bared, eyes staring, his hair in flaming red and orange spikes, scowling horribly at the photographer. We've got it propped up on the mantelpiece. Gran hates the sight of it.

Then again, when Crusher goes to all the trouble of shaving his head, Gran doesn't like that any better. She doesn't like his tattoo. I've even heard her telling our next-door neighbours how common she thinks it is. And they agreed. (They're not keen on Crusher, either. They don't like the noise his car makes when it starts – *if* it starts. They say it wakes their children.)

Personally, I rather like Crusher's tattoo. It only shows up when his head is freshly shaved. It says MADE IN BIRMINGHAM, and Crusher claims he was – well, on the outskirts. And we don't see it all that often anyway, because whenever he's gone to the trouble of dyeing his hair a different colour, he lets the spikes grow out all over.

Crusher dyes his hair pretty often, considering. Since the postcard, he's been green and pink, yellow and purple. Right now he's blue. Gran and he had a row about it only last week. Crusher just happened to stroll into the kitchen while Gran was tipping breakfast plates into the sink and washing them, so we could start on the tea. Mum was upstairs, doing something in the bathroom, no one knew what, but it was using up all the hot water, Gran said. And I was giving Crummy Dummy her bottle.

"Wotcha, Granny," Crusher greeted her cheerily. "I hope one of those plates you're rinsing is for me."

He's ever so friendly, is Crusher Maggot. I can't think why Gran just can't get used to him, like I did. But she can't. She spun round at the draining-board and glowered at him before saying tartly:

"You've got your feet well and truly under the table, haven't you, young Maggot?"

Baffled, Crusher looked down at his Doc Martens. Gran kept on at him. She's good at nagging, Gran is. (Mum says that I take after her.)

"Look at your hair!" Gran snorted. "It's sky blue! It's dreadful the way you amble around this estate looking like something that fell off the wall at the Modern Art Gallery. I'm horrified that a daughter of mine is prepared even to be seen walking along the street beside someone with hair that shocking colour!"

"Your hair is blue, too," argued Crusher. He was hurt. "You had that perm and rinse and set only last week. Your hair is definitely blue."

"A faint bluish tinge, maybe," Gran said, blushing hotly. "Not sky blue!"

"Not royal blue, either!" I cried, for Mum had just sailed into the kitchen. And her hair was royal blue! It was the brightest, deepest, richest blue I ever saw. It was bluer than winter afternoons, bluer than the leggings Gran knitted for Crummy Dummy, bluer even than Sophie Howard's gown when she played the Virgin Mary in our Nativity play last year.

Gran stared. I stared. Crusher stared. Even Crummy Dummy stared. Then Gran and Crummy Dummy both burst into tears.

"Waaaah!" screamed Crummy Dummy, and she stretched out her arms desperately to me, hoping I would protect her from this blue-topped stranger.

"Aaaaagh!" shrieked poor Gran, holding her hand over her heart. Gingerly, she stuck out a finger and prodded one of Mum's spikes.

"How can you do this to your old mother?" she wailed. "A girl's hair is supposed to be her crowning glory! Royal-blue hair! *Royal-blue hair!* What will the neighbours think? Answer me that!"

"They'll think she looks fair smashing," said Crusher. "And that she matches the paintwork on my car."

You could tell Gran was shocked. She went pale as a grub.

"I'm warning you two," she said in her dangerous voice. "You're going too far. A mother can only stand *so much.*"

(This interested me. A lot. For I suspect my mum can stand almost any amount. It's me who cracks. That's why I have a lot of natural sympathy for my gran.)

Gran shook her finger at Mum so hard that her new perm and set wobbled on her head like a pale-blue jelly.

"If you stay royal blue, I shall disown you. Yes, I shall. I won't come round here any more. I won't babysit for you when you go down to the disco with this – this *barbarian* here" (pointing at Crusher, who looked hurt again). "I won't talk to you. I'll even cut you dead in the street. You have to choose. Royal-blue hair, or your own mother!"

There was a horrible silence. Nobody moved. Nobody spoke. Mum just looked sulky.

Gran turned to me. Prising Crummy Dummy out of my arms, she placed a kiss upon her forehead.

"Farewell, sweet babe," she said. "I hope for your sake that your mother sees sense, and we are not parted for too long."

I got a kiss and a speech too.

"Goodbye, Minna dear," she said. "I know it can be hard when a mother puts maggots before the family."

I had some sympathy with that, as well. I've thought it often enough myself, when Mum and Crusher are too wrapped up in giggling together about something silly to pay any attention to me.

"Bye, Gran," I said. "I, too, hope our parting won't last for long."

It did, though. It lasted for days. Gran never visited once. I was pretty upset, I can tell you. I missed her coming over every afternoon and asking me about what happened at school, and helping me with my spelling homework. And Crummy Dummy missed her too, you could tell. She took to sitting forlornly with her dummy in her mouth, looking all miserable and deprived.

On Wednesday, we caught sight of Gran for the first time since the quarrel. She was stepping out of Mr Hamid's shop carrying a bagful of vegetables just as we came over the pedestrian walkway to the shopping centre. I waved and shouted at her through the railings; but since I was with Mum, Gran ignored me and swept off under the concrete arches extremely grandly, like the Queen Mother, pretending she hadn't heard me call.

"See where your stubbornness has led us?" I scolded Mum, as Gran disappeared between Vikki's Video Palace and the boarded-up wool shop.

Mum said something rude. I shan't repeat it but I persisted in trying to reason with her.

"Is it worth it, just for blue hair?"

"Ask her, not me," snapped Mum, and pulled me after the pushchair so sharply she practically wrenched my arm out of its socket.

So I asked her. I asked Gran the very next time that I bumped into her, picking her way around the muddy patch of the shortcut across the recreation ground.

I spread my hands out in what the author of *My Best Bible Stories* always refers to as a "beseeching fashion".

"Is it worth it, Gran, just for blue hair?" I cried.

What Gran said was almost as rude as what Mum said. I shan't repeat that, either. But I confess to being a little shocked. She is my granny, after all.

I left the two of them to it, after that. I knew the problem couldn't last for ever because Crusher had told me Mum's blue was the sort that washed out. So I concentrated my efforts on cheering Crummy Dummy, who didn't know that. I made Crusher fix up her baby-bouncer. It's not been right since Mum took off half the chain links to wear to a dance. And I made the hole in her bottle a whole lot bigger. She's been sucking and blowing like a smoker when the lift's broken, trying to get the milk out, poor thing. I also cut the feet off the ends of her stripy babygrow suit. I reckon her toes were getting all squashed up.

And I waited ... but Gran never came, and Mum never even went next door to phone her. It was nearly a week.

"What a stubborn pair of bats!" was the only remark Crusher made about the whole sorry business.

Then, just as I was despairing, there came the night of the gale.

What a night that was! The rain beat down, lashing against the window panes till every dream turned into a nightmare. It was still dark at breakfast-time. Storm water was seeping under the kitchen door, and running over the lino in rivulets. The wind was so fierce it would have had Crummy Dummy's bonnet off in a flash, if I hadn't insisted Mum leave her with old Mrs Pitopoulos next door, instead of dragging her out in the pushchair.

"I don't *need* chumming to school," I told Mum when she was still scouring the cupboards hopelessly for her scarlet plastic bosun's helmet at seven minutes to nine. "You don't have to come with me."

"You don't *have* to go," she countered irritably.

"I do," I insisted. "It's a schoolday, isn't it? I'm not sick, or injured, am I?"

"Don't push your luck, Minna," she said, climbing into her wellies and scowling.

So we set off to school through the gale. You've never seen anything like it. The street was absolutely clean! All the litter had been washed away – even the tatty old cardboard boxes outside number twelve, and those great lengths of stair carpet on the corner that the dustbin men have refused for four whole weeks to shove into their mechanical chewer.

The main road was amazing, too. Cars were crawling along with their drivers hunched forward and peering through little arcs on the windscreens. The tyres hurled wide sheets of filthy gutter water up in our faces. Mum spat and cursed. Her wellies were flooded.

And just at that moment, I noticed Gran. She was staggering out of her cul-de-sac, into the wind, fighting her umbrella which looked just as though it were fighting her back.

I squeezed Mum's arm.

"Look," I said, pointing. "Gran! And we're going the same way."

Mum blinked raindrops off her eyelashes, and looked. Then she shouted to me over the wind:

"I'm not slowing up. Not in this weather. And now I'm this wet, I'm not going back either."

And, with that, she strode on with her head down against the spiteful winds and the rain.

Gran was striding along, almost beside us. She clearly had the same idea. The weather was far too awful to slow up, or take a longer route, or go back home and set off again later. She was going to brazen it out, just like Mum.

The two of them were practically side by side now, each striding along into the wind, and neither of them so much as giving one tiny little sideways peep at the other.

And that was their big mistake! For the oddest thing was happening. The strangest sight! Both of them were changing. It was almost as if the storm were playing its own little private joke on the pair of them.

Mum's hair was changing back to its normal colour! First, little streaks started running like tiny bright-blue rivers down her cheeks, over her ears, and down the back of her neck. Her hair was gradually returning to mousey-brown, the colour it was before she went royal blue. The dye was washing out, faster and faster. And the spikes were collapsing. The wind was blowing them flat. Mum didn't notice, but by the time we reached the corner, she looked as clean and neat and tidy as she does in the photo that was taken of her at convent school.

(Gran loves that photo. She keeps it on the mantelpiece at her house in a special fur frame. Mum says it makes her look like a wally, and slams it down on its face whenever we visit. If the frame wasn't fur, she'd have smashed it by now, doing that.)

And Mum wasn't the only one looking different. Gran was changing, too. As she marched into the same fierce wind, her neat little parting was whipped away, and patches of her hair stuck up in clumps, like Crusher's after his football practice. Her hair was wet, too, making the blue look bluer. Gran no longer looked like someone who'd been to the hairdresser only ten days ago. She looked like someone who'd been dragged backwards through a hedge.

Then, as we reached the school gates, the wind gave one last, amazing flourish. It whipped Gran's hair up into spikes. It whipped a nice neat parting into Mum's straight brown hair. And it whipped the umbrella clean out of Gran's grasp.

Mum reached out and caught the handle automatically, as it flew past. Then, since she couldn't think of anything else to do with it, she turned to Gran to hand it back.

Gran turned to her, to take it.

Both of them stared.

Gran stared at neat, sweet, tidy Mum, looking just like she used to look in her favourite photo on the mantelpiece.

Mum stared at punky, spiky, blue Gran, looking a bit like Crusher Maggot on a bad morning.

Tears came to Gran's eyes first.

"Look at you! You look *lovely!*" she cried, and reached out to give Mum one of her giant hugs.

"And you!" Mum squealed with pleasure, hugging her back. "You look smashing, just smashing!"

"What a wonderful surprise!"

"Oh, you are too! Really!"

I sighed, and shook my head. Then the school bell rang. I walked away, and neither of them even noticed. They were far too busy praising one another for their beautiful hairstyles.

It's a good job there are no mirrors hanging on our school wall, I reckoned. But you never know … In my experience, most of their silly squabbles get sorted out in time, if you just ignore them.

Karate for Kids

by Terence Blacker

You're probably not going to believe this. Pretty soon you'll be saying, *Oh please. Gimme a break. Pull the other one, guy.*

So maybe I had better just lay it on you straight, no messing.

My name is Kick.

Better known to my readers as *Karate for Kids*.

Better known to Miss Brown, the librarian, as SL10473 (Sports and Leisure Section).

You there yet? Right. Got it? Fact is, I'm a book – 192 pages, hardback, with a picture on the front of some geeky guy wearing pyjamas and waving his hands about.

Surprised, huh? There you were, thinking that books just lay around the place, getting read and gathering dust, when up jumps old Kick and starts telling you about walking books and talking books and party dude books.

Books that now and then have had it up to here with being taken for granted. Books who decide to do something about it.

Right? Right.

Now shut up and listen.

Picture the scene. The Weston Street Library – a small, friendly sort of place, kind of scuffed but kind of homely. In one corner there's the children's library. Along the back wall is the newspaper section. Near the door (some of the old-timers would like them *outside* the door) there's a rack of videos and tapes.

It's the end of the day, right? Miss Brown goes round switching off the lights. She hesitates for a moment. "Night, guys," she says quietly (we like that). Then she leaves, locking the door.

Silence. Darkness. Then, after about fifteen or twenty minutes, a sound.

"Psst."

"Ssh!"

"Ssh yourself."

"Has she gone?"

"Duh. Only about an hour ago."

"Sheesh, what a day I've had."

"Me, too."

Soon the place is alive with voices – loud, soft, rude, polite, every kind of accent. We move off our shelves, ruffle our pages, stretch our spines, go visit a friend, catch up on the news.

By the middle of the night, it's party time at the Weston Street Library. In one corner, the Enid Blytons will be having yet another of their picnics. Over there, the Roald Dahls will be preparing a stinkbomb. Maybe the Anne Fines and the Judy Blumes will get together to talk about relationships.

Me, I'll be hanging out with my two best buddies, Snog and Drill – chatting, rapping and generally shooting the breeze.

Let me introduce them to you. Snog's real name is *Love's Sweet Mystery*. She's about a million pages long and her cover shows a historical couple in a clinch (hence her nickname, which she hates, by the way).

Drill is big, fat, heavy and kind of dull-looking (though no one's dared tell him this to his front cover). His real name is *The Complete A-to-Z Companion to Basic Home Decorating*.

OK, so we're kind of an odd bunch, but then friends are like that, right? Sometimes you seem to have nothing in common with your buddies except the fact that you like each other.

Let me tell you what brought Snog, Drill and me together. We have this one thing in common: when we're taken out by readers, each of us has a tough time.

Take Drill. Because the guy's a bit tubby (488 pages and big with it) there always comes a moment when his reader will use him to stand on. Or to prop up a work-bench. Now and then he's even been used as a hammer.

With Snog, it's different. She gets the nicely-spoken ladies. By Chapter 10 (lover-boy hero has to go off to war, blahdy-blah), her pages are getting a bit tear-stained. By Chapter 18 (lover boy reported killed in the war, boo-hoo), she's getting damper all the time. By the last chapter (lover boy not really killed, all a terrible mistake, comes home, hurray-hurray, kissy-kissy, happy ever after), she's awash. I tell you, sometimes when Snog gets back to her shelf, she looks as if she's been dropped in the municipal swimming pool.

And me? Have you any idea what it's like being *Karate for Kids*? They take you home. They read you, they study you, they learn that, before a person tries breaking a brick with their bare hands, that person should always practise on something softer. Hm, something softer, eh? You can almost hear the brain ticking (face it, I don't get the brightest readers). Then at last they get it.

They lay me down carefully, so that I'm like a bridge between two other books.

I brace myself.

Hiiiii-YAH!

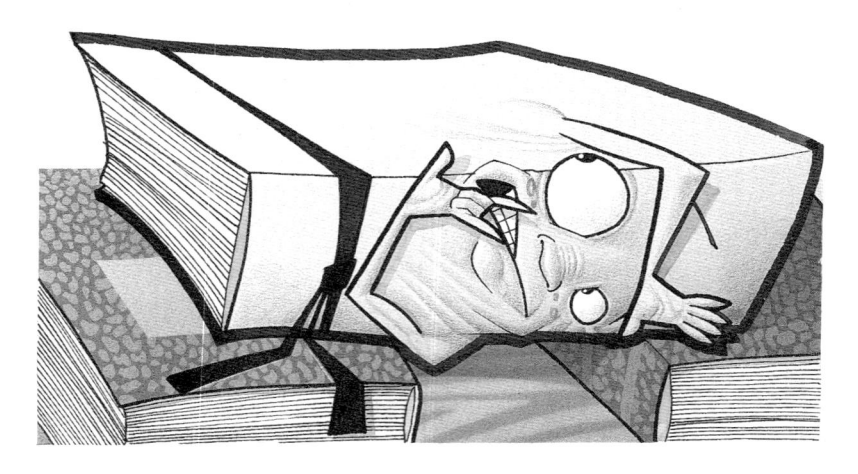

Crunch! Right down my spine. It's not the discomfort I mind (hey, they don't call us hardbacks for nothing), it's the ingratitude. The better I've taught them, the more they hurt me. Go figure.

So it's the Kick-Snog-Drill gang, right? Now and then we josh each other about things — Drill being a bit slow, Snog whiffing of her readers' cheap perfume, or me talking in a kind of phoney American accent (I was printed in Colchester, but my soul belongs to Colorado) — but, at the end of the day when the lights go down, we're there for each other.

And we needed to be, the day they decided to close down the Weston Street Library.

Get this. One night, it's shutting-up time at the library. Except it doesn't shut up. And Miss Brown, who's looking even paler than usual, seems kind of agitated.

Now we've seen this look before. (Between you and me, she's not as quiet as she looks. Sometimes when she gets telephone calls after closing time, we hear conversations that would make your pages curl.) But tonight's different.

Five minutes after closing time, she gets two visitors. One is Mrs Knights, the Chief Leisure Officer from the council. The other's a nerdy little guy in a suit they call Mr Johnson. Mrs Knights makes small talk with Miss Brown. The geek wanders around the shelves looking like he's been forced to visit a rubbish dump.

My bookish instinct tells me that this guy ain't no reader.

"Monster property," he mutters to himself now and then. "Monster investment opportunity."

He returns to the desk where Mrs Knights and Miss Brown are standing.

"These will make excellent one-bedroom properties," he says. "Complete with luxury kitchenette and full en-suite facilities. A dream home for the young, single, professional person."

All round the shelves, we're pricking up our pages. Did he just say "Dream home"?

"Of course, closure of the library still has to be confirmed," says Mrs Knights. "We've got the public meeting tomorrow."

Johnson laughs nastily "Yeah, yeah. Monster publicity exercise, then we go ahead, right?"

"This library is important." At last Miss Brown speaks up. "It's the only one in the area. How are people going to get books and information if it's closed down?"

"Like, get in a car and drive?" says the geek.

"What about children? What about old people?" Miss Brown seems on the point of tears. "Isn't reading a right for them too?"

"Nah, books are old-fashioned."

Miss Brown is about to reply but the property man is sidling up to her.

"Tell you what, darling," he murmurs. "Maybe we can get you a place at the front of the queue for one of the flats. Do you a monster deal, babe."

I don't want a monster deal," hisses Miss Brown angrily. "I want a library."

"I'm sure your personal views will be listened to with great interest at tomorrow's meeting." Mrs Knights glances at her watch impatiently. "Now, if you'll excuse me, I've got a council meeting."

"I wonder if I could take a few moments to make some measurements." Old monster man has taken a tape-measure out of his pocket. "It'll only take five minutes."

"Of course," says the Chief Leisure Officer. "Would you mind, Miss Brown?"

"Mind?" Our librarian is staring into space. Something catches her eye. It's me. Cool as you like, I move an inch or so down the shelf. Suddenly a distant smile is on Miss Brown's lips. "No, of course I don't mind. I'll just go and lock the side-door."

52

And as she makes her way past us, we hear her mutter, "Over to you, guys." (Did I mention to you that Miss Brown knows about our secret lives? Sheesh, of *course* she does. Librarians understand books – that's what they *do*.)

Little geeky Johnson is down on his knees, measuring the length of one wall, whistling to himself when we hear the side-door being locked. Moments later, we see Miss Brown pass the window outside the library. The lock on the front door turns quietly.

"Monster, monster, monster, babe." The geek snaps his notebook shut, stands up and looks around him. "Babe? Miss Brown?"

He walks to the side-door. As he rattles the lock unsuccessfully, one of the guys in the wildlife section – maybe *The Hodder Book of European Birds*, but I'm not sure – takes wing. Silent as an owl in flight, he floats across the room and bangs into the light switches on the far wall.

53

Johnson returns to a library in darkness. "Yeah, great joke, Miss Brown." There's a hint of panic in his voice. "Hit the light, babe. I'm monster afraid of the dark."

No reply. Bumping into shelves, swearing to himself, he edges his way to the front door. He turns the handle. Pulls the door with increasing desperation. For what seems like several minutes, he hammers on the heavy wooden door.

It's when he stops that he first becomes aware that he's not alone.

Drill makes the first move. Fact is, it's about the only move he can make, but right now it works the trick big-time. He leans back on his shelf and lets himself fall to the floor.

Bang!

"Who's that?" Johnson's voice is a squawk. He starts to blunder towards the window – then stops.

Like a marching army the whole encyclopaedia section makes its way out of Reference and ranges itself across the floor, barring his passage.

"Monster weird, man." Johnson backs away, his eyes wide with alarm. "Aagh, what was that?"

The Hodder Book of European Birds has taken wing again, fluttering past his face.

As he turns, Snog surprises us all by scurrying across the floor, tripping him as she goes.

55

In the darkness, we watch Johnson crawling on his hands and knees. For some reason, I find myself thinking of all the times my readers have practised their karate chops on me. That's the thing with me – I can resist anything but temptation.

"Whack!" I swoop down and catch him a superb *haichindo* kick, knocking him flat on his face.

From the shelves all around me can be heard the other books ruffling their pages. *What* had he said? Books are *old-fashioned*? It was time Mr Johnson experienced a bit of book-learning at first hand.

Thirty minutes or so later, Johnson manages to reach the central desk and telephones the police.

By the time the cops have opened up the library, we're back on our shelves, innocent as pie.

And Johnson? They find him under a table. His suit's torn, his eyes are darting this way and that, and he seems to be having trouble speaking.

"What exactly is the trouble, sir?" asks one of the policemen.

After a few seconds he finds the words. "M-m-monster books," he whispers.

"Yes, of course, sir." The policeman helps him to his feet. "Books are rather monster, aren't they? I like a good read myself."

* * *

Fast forward. The next evening, Weston Street Library is full of chairs and the chairs are full of people. I catch sight of several of Snog's whiffy ladies, maybe one or two of Drill's DIY experts. There are some of my readers, cracking their knuckles as Mrs Knights, Johnson and Miss Brown take their places.

Mrs Knights makes a little speech. No more money, yahdy-yah, cuts in council spending, yahdy-yah, lots of other libraries in the borough, yahdy-yahdy-yah.

"But you know what they say." She smiles brightly. "When one door closes, another one opens." She turns to Johnson. "I'd like to introduce you all to the council's property consultant, Gavin Johnson. He's going to tell you how these premises will help another important area for the borough – housing."

Johnson gets to his feet. "Thank you, Mrs Knights," he says politely. He looks around him, and in that moment there isn't a book in the room that's not thinking that we've failed – the geek is back to his own self.

"Let me put it this way," he says. "What does this borough need most? Monster savings in its budget and superbly designed one-bedroom flats in the brand new Library Apartment block, or a load of mouldy old books that you can find down the road in one of the other libraries or in a bookshop?"

There are mutterings from the readers in front of him.

"The answer, of course, is books." He sits down again, quickly.

For a few seconds, there's an astonished silence in the library.

Mrs Knights is the first to react. "I beg your pardon?" she says. "You're meant to be our property consultant. What about the kitchenettes, the full en-suite facilities?"

Johnson shrugs, and gives a slightly embarrassed smile. "Last night I spent a bit of quality time with the books in the library," he says. "I've had a monster change of mind. To tell the truth, this place would never have made very good flats, anyway."

I've never seen Miss Brown look so happy. "Does this mean the library will stay open?" she asks.

Arms crossed, Mrs Knights is still staring at Johnson. "It rather looks as if it will," she murmurs.

Suddenly there's applause from all around the room. Readers of all ages are smiling with relief, Miss Brown is blushing, even old Mrs Knights and Mr Johnson seem to be enjoying their rare moment of popularity, as if, in their heart of hearts, they know that the right decision has been made.

And if you listen very carefully, you might just hear some other sounds.

Like Drill, riffling his big pages in approval.

Like Snog, sniffing emotionally.

Like, maybe even your old pal Kick, the hardest hardback in Weston Street Library, stretching his spine in celebration.

Tell the truth, I'm kind of choked up right now just thinking about it.

And, hey, why not?

Books are people too, right?

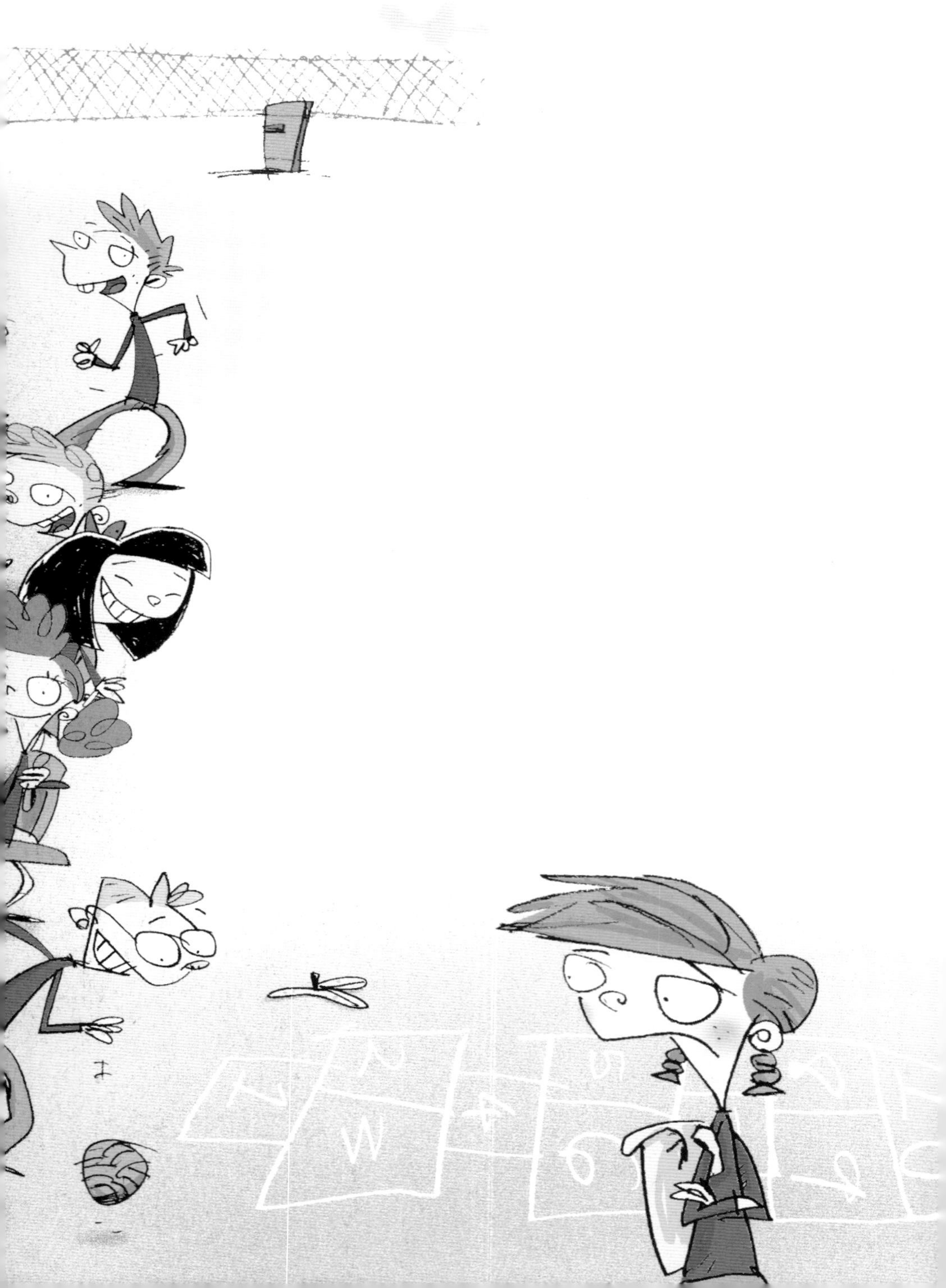

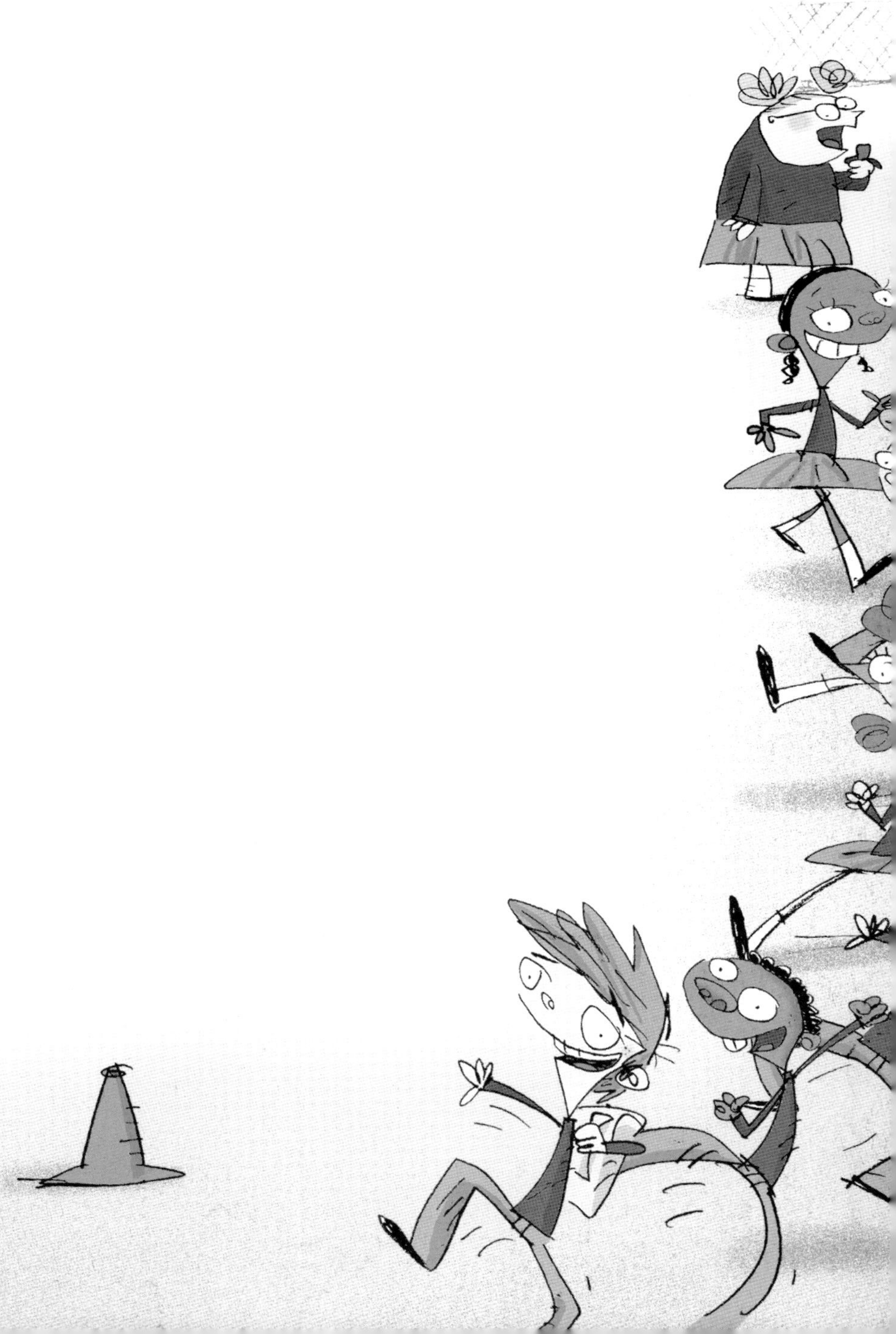

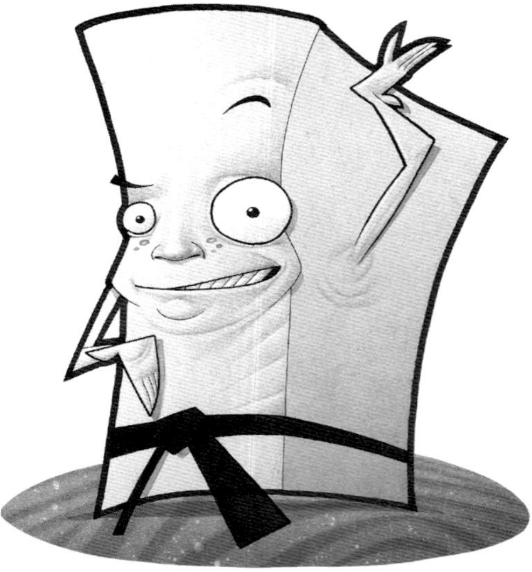